Aurea Vidyā Collection*

———— 14 ————

*For a complete list of Titles, see page 101.

Published by Aurea Vidyā
39 West 88th Street, New York, N.Y. 10024
www.vidya-ashramvidyaorder.org

This book was originally published in Italian as
Raphael, *La Via del Fuoco Secondo la Qabbālāh*, 'Ehjeh 'Ašer
'Ehjeh, by Edizioni Āśram Vidyā, Roma, Italy 1978
Third Edition, 1999

First published in English in 1993 as
Raphael, *Pathway of Fire*, Initiation to the Kabbalah, by
Samuel Weiser, Inc., York Beach, ME, U.S.A.

©Āśram Vidyā 1978
English Translation ©Āśram Vidyā 1993/2012

Set in font ©Vidyā 11/13 points by Aurea Vidyā

Printed and bound by Lightning Source Inc. at locations in the
U.S.A. and in the U.K., as shown on the last page

ISBN   10: 1-931406-14-6   13: 978-1-931406-14-7
Library of Congress Control Number: 2012916004

On the Cover: "Melchizedek and Abraham", plate in gold and enamel
by Nicholas de Verdun, Klosterneuburg (XII century). Melchizedek
is authentic representative of the Primordial Tradition: the
"Eternal Sacerdos" (*Psalm* 110, 4), "Without genealogy" because
of "non-human" origin, who combines in his person both the
sacerdotal and regal functions stemming from the one Principle.

Raphael

'Ehjeh 'Ašer 'Ehjeh

(I am That I am)

THE PATHWAY OF FIRE
ACCORDING TO THE QABBĀLĀH

AUREA VIDYĀ

«... Comprehend and you will know... Ten Sephiroth, save the Ineffable, their end is joined with their principle like the flame with the burning coal. Only the Lord is above them and has no second».

Sepher Yezirah

TABLE OF CONTENTS

FOREWORD

The Hebrew term *Qabbālāh*, which is equivalent to the the word *Māsôrāh*, means "reception" or "transmission", and represents the esoteric part of the Old Testament. This means that the Old Testament, besides having an external and exoteric function, has also a deeper and significant function which is internal and esoteric.

In *Pirqe Ābot* I, 1 of the *Talmūd* we read:

«Moses received the Law (*Torāh*) upon Mount Sinai and transmitted it to Joshua, Joshua transmitted it to the Elders, the Elders to the Prophets and the Prophets to the Great Congregation».

Thus, Moses is the first link in the chain of the cabalistic Tradition which "received" the *Māsôrāh* from the divine Voice-Sound.

In its complete form the *Qabbālāh* can be divided into two parts that correspond to two precise points of view: one includes the unfolding of the universal manifestation, and from this point of view is similar to the *darśana Sāṁkhya* (this term, like that of *Sephirah*, means "numeration"); the second includes the metaphysical point of view of Ain Soph where everything is seen as emptiness or as simple fleeting phenomenon.

Ain Soph may be compared to the *Turīya* of *Vedānta*, whereas the *Qabbālāh* may, in general, be said to be a synthesis of *Sāṁkhya* and *Advaita Vedānta*, although within it, the vision of the latter remains veiled.

'Ehjeh Ašer 'Ehjeh means "I am That I am", "Being is Being", "I am Who I am", and is the Divine answer to Moses' question on Mount Sinai to know what His name might be.

This utterance may be compared also to the upanishadic *mantra*: "I am That " or "I am *Brahman* (*Aham brahmāsmi*) ".

Raphael's aphorisms aim at making a simple contribution toward cabalistic realization and, above all, they are meant for those who, wishing to emerge from the strictly magical viewpoint (in its various aspects) from which the *Qabbālāh* is usually considered, seek to reach initiatory realization, which is the ultimate goal of the cabalistic Tradition.

Aurea Vidyā

THE SEPHIROTHIC TREE

1. The sephirothic tree is a *maṇḍala*, a symbol in which the numberless expressive possibilities of the micro-macrocosm are summarized.

Therefore its proper interpretation reveals the meaning of the world of names and forms, gives an understanding of the gross and subtle energies and the possibilities of grasping them.

It may be "meditated" at a metaphysical, ontological, theurgical or psychological level.

Being a complete *maṇḍala* it is a symbol of noetic Reality.

2. A symbol represents the reality that lies behind representations; in other words, behind every phenomenon, appearance (*māyā*) or form we find a universal creating principle, though invisible and sensorially intangible. Thus, the transcendent reality may manifest itself in an immanent manner by means of a symbol. From this point of view the formal world itself is the symbol of the metaphysical reality. The symbol does not identify itself with the principle it expresses, therefore, in order to grasp the principle, one must turn to intuition.

3. The error that the empirical mind (*manas*) normally makes is that of confining itself to a conceptual interpretation of the symbol, depriving it of the principle it manifests. The mind, therefore, interprets empty shells.

The empirical imaginative mind not only estranges us from the reality that the symbol proposes, but it causes us to degrade and materialize the symbol itself to such a degree as to confine life to the world of shadows and appearances.

4. The Tree, which represents the basis of the *Qabbālāh* is a Pathway to realization. By meditating on and contemplating it one may realize the world of Principles, its vital expression, the pathway of descent (solidification) and that of re-ascent (solution).

To reduce the Tree to a simple magical handbook suitable for magicians means debasing It and emptying It of Its true contents and, moreover, giving the denigrators of the Tradition a good chance for cheering up.

On the other hand, one must recognize the fact that many disciples and scholars of the Tree fail to go beyond its material and psychical aspects and that all their attention is centered exclusively upon the sephirah Yesod, that is the sphere of sexual polarity, emptied of its intrinsic reality which, as a symbol, is there to demonstrate.

5. One must consider two aspects of the Tree: involutionary and evolutionary. However, it would be good to banish these terms from an initiatory context, wherefore we shall talk of: fall and re-ascension, dreaming and awakening, downward and upward journey, and outward and inward movement.

If we consider the Tree under its realizative aspect, it must be proposed from the point of view of its re-ascending or awakening function because Initiation involves a consciential expansion of principial and universal factors, which can obviously be found in their own sphere.

Thus, if we wish to speak of Initiation – and not of mere sexual or psychological magic – we must agree that the task of the disciple who approaches the Tree without ambiguity is that of "awakening" to the consciousness of Tiphereth first and then, finally, to that of Kether.

We must not forget that Adam is a... fallen and stunned God, and that his task is that of recovering his primeval condition. From this stems the conception of "Awakening ".

6. «Ten (excluding the Ineffable Ain) and not nine, ten and not eleven; understand and you will know», says the *Sepher Yezirah*, «exert your intuition upon them, seek, discriminate, take note and set things back in their proper places, and place the Creator upon His throne».

«Ten sephiroth, save the Ineffable; their aspect is like that of dazzling flames, their fulfillment is to be found in the infinite. Through them the Word of God is revealed: by ceaselessly externalizing and internalizing themselves like whirlwinds of fire they fulfill the divine Word bowing before the throne of the Eternal.

Ten sephiroth, save the Ineffable; their end is joined with their principle like the flame with the burning coal; only the Lord is above them and has no second.

What other number can you utter before the number One?».

7. «According to the most prestigious Rabbis, it seems that Moses himself, foreseeing the fate that his book might meet and the false interpretations it might undergo in time, took recourse to a spoken law which he transmitted orally to a number of trustworthy disciples, and that he gave them the task of transmitting it in the secrecy of the sanctuary to other men who in turn would transmit it from age to age so

as to have it come down to remote posterity. This oral law... is called *Qabbālāh*, from the Hebrew word which means "what has been received", "what is passed from hand to hand "»[1].

There are two written scripts that may be considered as the basis of the *Qabbālāh*: the *Zohar* (Splendor) and the *Sepher Yezirah* (Numeration); they contain the Old Testament's esoteric Teaching.

8. If the Tree includes *also* a theurgical aspect, this term must be taken to mean *theós* = God, *ergon* = work, activity. Theurgy is not meant for practical, material, immediate or utilitarian ends or things of this kind, but for union with the Divine, and the deification and immortality of the human being.

In space-time the consciousness of the individual has become increasingly metalized, constraining itself more and more within the confines of the material and psychic spheres.

The Western esoteric Tradition has gradually lost impact and ground (although it never died; a Tradition cannot die, it may become veiled and obscured or it may withdraw) because the men to whom it was directed have forgotten the Principle, the metaphysical sphere, from which all things draw their origin and nourishment.

A culture and a science that lose this point of view, or rather, that stray from the metaphysical Principle cannot but perish because they have no basis upon which to rest.

All the traditional sciences have become degraded because their scholars have not taken into account the transcendent or metaphysical Principle. When knowledge is not based upon the

---

[1] Antoine Fabre d'Olivet, *La langue hébraïque restituée*. Dorbon-Aîné. Paris. (French Edition).

Principle it becomes technical (whether scientific or magical) and a set of facts, concepts and words.

9. Although the divine Expressions (Intelligences) are indefinite, nonetheless the Tree divides them into ten groups, because this number represents perfection. These divine Expressions are given the name of *sephiroth* in the plural form and of *sephirah* in the singular; the term means number or numeration.

The sephiroth are, therefore, the keys that open the doors to divine Knowledge and to the *practical utilization* of such Knowledge. They are hierarchical Powers that operate in the intra-individual and the universal. It is important therefore to consider the Number, the Idea-Intelligence and the Name: we shall return to these concepts later.

10. In *Isaiah* (11, 2) we read:

«Above Him will rest the spirit of the Lord, the spirit of wisdom (Chokmah) and intelligence (Binah), the spirit of counsel (Chesed) and strength (Geburah), the spirit of science and pity (Tiphereth)... »

And in *Chronicles* or *Paralipomenon* (I, 29, 11):

«Yours, oh Lord, is magnificence (Chesed), power (Geburah), beauty (Tiphereth), victory (Nezach) and glory (Hod); because all that is in heaven and on earth is yours (Yesod = basis of everything); yours, oh Lord, is the kingdom (Malkuth) and you are above all kings (Kether)»

«God, with Wisdom (Chokmah) created the earth, with Intelligence (Binah) he formed the skies. Due to his Science (Da'ath) the founts spring forth and the clouds yield dew»

(*Proverbs*: III, 19-20)

11. The sephiroth are the archetypes, the essential determinations, the prime causes, the principles of all manifest things. Thus, they are not distinct, opposite, individual Entities, but they represent various aspects of the One Reality (Kether).

They are simple "modifications" of the divine Mind, they are cyphers of the sole Power that is the One (Kether). The Tree represents the Unity of manifest and non-manifest life.

To separate one sephirah from all the others giving it absolute value means misinterpreting, altering and falsifying the sephirothic *maṇḍala* and therefore the synthetical reality it contains.

12. A sephirah is an Idea, a Power-Substance, an Energy or a Strength, depending upon the point from which one may wish to observe it.

In the field of science one speaks of "force of gravity", "electronic energy", power of light, of law of inertia, etc. In other words, the universe is governed by Forces, Laws and Principles; therefore the sephirothic *maṇḍala* represents Power-Forces or Intelligences, the Laws and the Principles.

A Law concerns the behavior of a Power-Force, or an Intelligence. When one understands the sephiroth-powers one also understands the subtle Laws that lie behind the gross world of names and forms which, in turn, represents the complexity of the elements of nature.

13. These Intelligence-Powers are called:

Ain Soph = What is beyond names and forms. Ain = nothing. The Absolute cannot be intended except in terms of "not this, not this"

Kether = A King's face seen from the side

Chokmah	=	The face of a bearded man
Binah	=	A beautiful corpulent woman
Chesed	=	A crowned King sitting upon his throne
Geburah	=	A warrior King in his war chariot
Tiphereth	=	A beautiful regal figure. An innocent child or a glorious man on a cross
Nezach	=	A splendid nude Venus
Hod	=	A hermaphrodite
Yesod	=	A nude corpulent man
Malkuth	=	A woman on a throne

14. As we said above, the sephiroth may be considered from various points of view.

From a philosophical point of view the sephiroth are Ideas, Archetypes, universal Principles that are beyond form and even beyond name. From a theological point of view, they represent the various divinities or the angelical Hierarchies of Kether, as the creating God, and may be classified as follows:

1.	*Kether*	=	Chajoth or Seraphs
2.	*Chokmah*	=	Ophanim or Cherubs
3.	*Binah*	=	Aralim or Thrones
4.	*Chesed*	=	Haschemalim or Dominations
5.	*Geburah*	=	Seraphs or Virtues
6.	*Tiphereth*	=	Malachim or Powers
7.	*Nezach*	=	Elohim or Principalities
8.	*Hod*	=	Ben Elohim or Archangels
9.	*Yesod*	=	Cherubs or Angels
10.	*Malkuth*	=	Ischim or Souls

From a universal psychological point of view they represent energetic qualities or vital psychic expressions.

From the formal physical point of view they represent interacting "substances"; thus Binah is the primordial elementary substance from which all gross, supra-physical subtle and noumenal bodies are made. Malkuth is, instead, the grossest substance from which the various physical-material body-elements are made. The sephiroth, therefore, constitute *substances* at various degrees of condensation, vibration and movement.

As we can see, the Tree may be studied from a physical, psychological, theurgical, philosophical point of view, and if we consider Ain Soph, also from a metaphysical point of view.

Whith reference to the Ways or Pathways there are correspondences with the metaphysical, the philosophical, theurgical, magical-occultist, etc., pathways.

SEX AND QABBĀLĀH

15. When certain sephiroth – see Nezach, Hod or Yesod – become separated from the Principle on which they depend and from which they derive their raison d'être, their own expressive movement becomes degenerated, depraved and altered, leading obviously to error, conflict and profound aberration. When, for example, the sephirah Yesod is not governed by the Principle, we have a pathological sex-maniacal degeneration typical of those who interpret life in a unilateral, neurotic and obsessive manner.

There are several works of "sexual magic" which prospect the acquisition of Powers or even union with the Absolute, proposing exclusively sexual activity or, rather, orgies; the more the orgy is free of subconscious, binding and repressive contents, the more it reveals Kether, the One, the universal, God/principle. This might lead one to think that Kether – the God-Person, the Lord of the world and of all worlds – and his Intelligences have a predilection above all for brothels that, among other things, belong to a certain individualized order. We have to set things clear: we do no wish to diminish certain normal existential activities, disown them or to denigrate them "moralistically". Nor do we wish, either, to deny the *polar* function that is to be found within the manifest and in particular within our expression of life. This is in order to avoid all misunderstandings. On the other hand, as it *includes* everything, a true metaphysical vision does not exclude anything, but makes everything depend upon the Principle.

16. It is necessary however to underline the fact that, for Tradition, polarity is inherent in the individual himself; thus, Adam has Eve within him (for the East, the individual is the polar expression of *Puruṣa* and *Śakti* which are placed spatially at the Center of the head and at the base of the spinal cord) and the *scission* occurred due to the "fall" itself.

That which is "scattered" (duality) must be united (unity) and unity is achieved when Eve is resolved into Adam or when *Śakti*, awakening, reunites with *Puruṣa*.

The doctrine of Tantrism, the one submitted to the Principle, teaches us that a man and a woman may operate within the sphere of Yesod so that a powerful concentration of *prāṇa* is determined within their auras, and by means of correct positions and appropriate techniques and visualizations, can awaken *Śakti* uniting it with *Puruṣa* or *Śiva*. Because it is a real union of which one speaks (rather than merely coupling in order to enjoy pleasure), this type of union excludes all kinds of gratifying elements. Only one who assumes the solar position and not the lunar one shall vanquish the great Goddess Kuṇḍālinī.

17. However, sex, as it is normally conceived, is the symbol of a more profound and more universal reality. But when the symbol loses its soul or the content that is innate to it, it remains but a shadow, the shell of itself void of expressive vitality.

Tradition expresses itself by means of symbols, *maṇḍalas* and pure ideas and, when the key to these symbols is lost, one makes use of amorphous skeletons, and representations invented by the restless and incomplete mind of unilateral individuality.

The sephirothic Tree is a *maṇḍala*-symbol and if one does not possess the key or the keys to its proper understanding one makes of the sephiroth a game subjected to vanity and individual weakness. And it is known that by placing the emphasis upon "certain aspects" (sex, acquisition of psychic powers of all kinds, etc.) one certainly attracts many followers.

The line of least resistance is for the majority, and it must be recalled that many are called but few are chosen. The "Narrow Doorway" is not for all, not because there are privileged or predestined persons but because not all wish to "die while living", not everyone wishes to "cease being" in order to Be.

STATES OF LIFE

18. As we have seen, the sephiroth are particularized expressions, although impersonal, of the Kether-Unity and, even though each sephirothic attribute has its own archetypical connotation or its own ontological *number*, its hierarchical grade and particular "influence", their essence or their noumenal life is identified with indivisible and unqualified Unity.

The sephiroth are simply shades of the one Color of the prnciple. A sephirah in itself and by itself can have neither existence nor influence; those who realize Kether synthesize sephirothic totality; for example, whoever realizes the Tiphereth consciousness synthesizes within himself the lower set of four (Nezach, Hod, Yesod and Malkuth).

The sephirothic whole is not "composed" of the various sephiroth: it is not quantity that forms Unity. The sephirothic whole is Unity itself in its own specific expression. The "Numerations" are simply spatial "points", and these points in turn are polarizations of the Point without dimension.

If one forgets all this, one falls into absolutistic particularism (with all the consequences of the case) which is an aberration of the empirical mind. which is unable to grasp totality-unity-synthesis.

19. According to the *Qabbālāh* manifestation is divided into four states or existential worlds which we shall now compare with the doctrine of *Vedānta*:

Qabbālāh	Vedānta
Aziluth	Turīya, nirguṇa Brahman
Briah	Īśvara
Yezirah	Hiraṇyagarbha
Assiah	Virāṭ

Aziluth is the sphere and the "root" of All, it is the Absolute and the substratum of formal and non-formal manifestation. A certain manifestation represents one of the infinite possible expressions of Aziluth. It is equivalent to the Ain Soph (the root of the Tree).

Briah is the creative sphere/principle, the cause of manifestation and the first determination of Aziluth on the non-formal plane.

Yezirah is the formative, animating sphere of subtle, archetypical manifestation; it represents the *anima mundi*, the universal plastic mediator.

Assiah is the corporeal sphere, that of prototypes and objectification.

All the sephiroth operate within these spheres and, in fact, they are their creating, animating and moulding Powers. A plane of life is the implementation of sephirothic energy. There are sephiroth which animate certain planes or certain spheres and sephiroth that give life to other levels. Therefore sephirothic unity is to be found in the harmonic decade that causes indefinite vital effects; every effect or prototype is connected to its sephirothic archetype-principle and through this very archetype to the One/principle or 'Ehjeh (I am).

From the point of view of the physical sciences, the sephiroth that operate in the three worlds represent: the vital *elements* of gross nature, the *energies* that move these elements and the *laws* ruling these energies and the sole *Principle* upon which all is based.

20. Briah is animated by the Kether-Chokmah-Binah triad; Yezirah by the Chesed-Geburah-Tiphereth one; and Assiah by the Nezach-Hod-Yesod triad.

Malkuth may be considered as being the sephirah of simple "precipitation". It is the world of effects, of "precipitates", of automatisms, it is not the world of causes or principles.

Aziluth, as cause of all causes, is therefore outside of any principle or causal determination.

21. Going on to the microcosm, the *Qabbālāh* considers the human being as a threefold unit, and that is:

– Neshāmāh (spirit)
– Rūah (soul)
– Nephesh (body)

If we wish to attune ourselves with the sephirothic world of Assiah (Nezach-Hod-Yesod-Malkuth) we must simply assume the sensorial-physical body as our support. If the tonal accord is to be achieved with the world of Yezirah (Chesed-Geburah-Tiphereth) we must rest on the support of Rūah, that is of one's own Soul or of the body of glory which is in us; and finally, if we wish to attune ourselves to the world of Briah (Kether-Chokmah-Binah) we need the support of Neshāmāh, our own spiritual Essence.

By making the appropriate correlations we have:

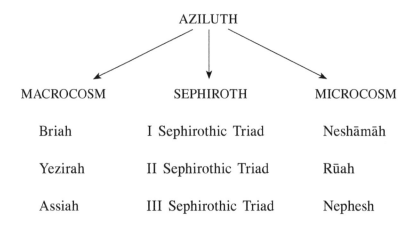

MACROCOSM	SEPHIROTH	MICROCOSM
Briah	I Sephirothic Triad	Neshāmāh
Yezirah	II Sephirothic Triad	Rūah
Assiah	III Sephirothic Triad	Nephesh

22. If one desires to "walk" with Chokmah or Chesed one must leave one's "shoes" at home. In His presence one must strip oneself of everything.

Whoever thinks that he can enter the sphere of the noumenal Fire, bringing with him his body of cells – perhaps even with its defects and particular desires – is mistaken. One who thinks that the universal mind can be realized while remaining within one's own particular and individualized mind, enters into irreducible contradiction. Whoever thinks that Unity can be realized while remaining attached to multiplicity, is fooling himself.

If one keeps in mind what has been said here, one can understand why many followers of the *Qabbālāh* operate within the sphere of Nezach-Hod and, above all, within that of Yesod, divorced from their superior principles.

23. The three sephirothic triads can be related to four speculative aspects: the metaphysical, the ontological, the psychological and the physiological.

I Triad	Kether Chokmah Binah	{ Principial ontological sphere Knowledge of identity *Mens informalis* (unitary Principle)
II Triad	Chesed Geburah Tiphereth	{ Archetypical universal sphere Intuitive Knowledge (Archetypes)
III Triad	Nezach Hod Yesod	{ The psychological and psychic sphere Empirical-sensorial cognition (Plastic mediator)
	Malkuth	{ The physical-corporeal sphere The five perceptive organs

The sphere of Ain Soph is concerned with pure metaphysics. And so the Tree, in its completeness, embraces the totality of Knowledge. Every higher sphere comprehends the lower one; therefore the metaphysical vision comprehends the totality of the points of view of knowing. Every sphere unveils certain Powers and Faculties that are particular to the sephiroth considered.

SEPHIROTHIC COLUMNS AND TRIADS

24. The Tree appears in the following symbolical configuration (see page 30).

25. First of all we have to emphasize a fact: the Tree is
composed of three columns, three pillars which represent the
"skeleton" and which here, for convenience's sake, shall be
called A, B and C.

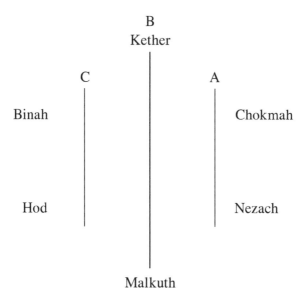

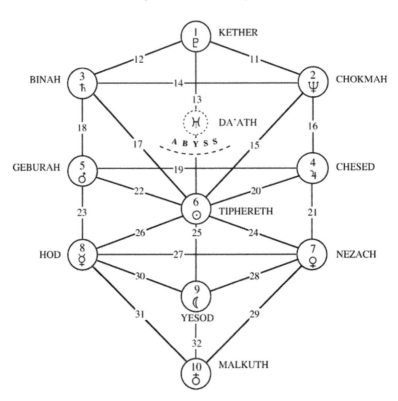

From the point of view of physics, A represents Energy and Strength; C represents the Element of nature and B the Law. From the psychological point of view, column A stands for conservation, clemency, mercy, benevolence; column C for rigor and creative activity; while B is concerned with synthesis, consciousness and balance. A and C are functions, faculties or powers that carry out activities; B, on the other hand, is awareness, the assimilation of polar action. It is the most subjective way, the furnace where the polar directions are amalgamated, fused and reconciled. One speaks of polarity because A and C do not represent absolute duality, but a simple polarity (A = positive; C = negative) caused by B-Kether. In Kether – the God Person – all sephirothic polarities are resolved and the consciousness which finds itself within the middle course, operates therefore in terms of synthesis. One might say that polarity operates in an balanced manner when it is subject to the action of the central column, that is of the just law.

In terms of *Yoga* one has:

A = *pingalā*, masculine, sun, positive
C = *iḍā*, feminine, moon, negative
B = *suṣumṇā* (where the two currents, or *nāḍis*, *pingalā* and *iḍā* are resolved)

Other correlations are :

A = energy, *rajas*, air
C = form, *tamas*, water
B = life-consciousness, *sattva*, fire

The three pillars have a precise correspondence with the Hermes' Caduceus. What is said of the Tree may also be said of the Caduceus.

26. The left pillar represents the aspect of movement-action, the right-hand one the aspect of stimulus and propulsion. Binah is the night moving toward the dawn, Geburah is the dawn and Hod is the day. Binah, Geburah and Hod give "form" to the propulsive and undifferentiated energy of Chokmah, Chesed and Nezach.

The left-hand pillar may be represented also as follows:

Binah ⟶	Geburah ⟶	Hod
Point	Line	Plane
Life	Quality	Form
Substance	Intellect	Mind
Root of motion	Motion	Appearance
	Subject	Object

From a qualitative point of view the right-hand pillar stands for:

$$Chokmah \ = \ Will$$
$$Chesed \ = \ Love$$
$$Nezach \ = \ Activity$$

The Will is determined as a stimulus to "form", as a power-sound that sets in motion the "primordial waters" (Binah).

Love appears as proper polar relationship commensurate with life and universal justice. Love is proper tonal accord (Geburah).

Activity is determined as intelligent creativity (Hod).

The pillar at the center represents the synthesis of the polar aspect, the realizing into consciousness of the formal-qualitative faculties, the Axis of the world, the universal center, the Tree of Life, while the left-hand and right-hand ones represent the Tree of Knowledge of "good" and "evil" and the way of rigor and clemency, the way of the "powers".

As already said, when in the human being these powers are not under to the direction of the Principle we have "egotistic magic" or power at the service of the empirical ego.

27. The sephirothic complex is further divided into three triads:

Kether-Chokmah-Binah	= Life aspect
Chesed-Geburah-Tiphereth	= Quality aspect
Nezach-Hod-Yesod	= Appearance, form aspect.

Malkuth, the tenth sephirah represents the plane of precipitations, objectivity and appearance; it is, as we have already seen, a simple effect.

Thus, on the opposite side, there is Ain Soph which is the strictly metaphysical, unqualified, non-manifest principle. On the one hand the densest objectivity and materiality, on the other the most rarefied subjectivity and essence: Alpha and Omega.

The first triangle is non-formal and non-manifest, although principial-causal. The second is the subtle universal animator; the third is of the individualized psychical order. Thus we have: the point, the line and the plane.

A triad is an operative unit upon a specific existential plane.

28. Every triad is formed by a polar aspect and by a point of synthesis, harmony and objective expression, wherefore, for example, one may obtain this type of triangulation:

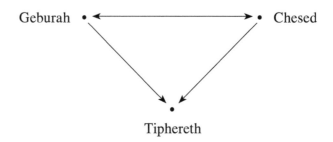

When there is an exchange of energy between Chesed and Geburah, Tiphereth is illuminated revealing the potentialities of the positive and negative aspects of the two sephiroth. Therefore, in our case, Tiphereth is the expressive vehicle of the Chesed-Geburah polar combination.

29. We have said that the sephirothic triads operate upon certain existential levels, therefore it is necessary to be very careful, when following the Way of *total* awakening, not to get lost along the path. One must comprehend that which is gross-material, that which is subtle-energetic, that which is essentially of the principle and, finally, that which is exclusively of metaphysical order.

In order to have a precise idea of the Way of Return it seems appropriate to propose an explicative table of the triads, proceeding from the bottom toward the top and leaving out Malkuth.

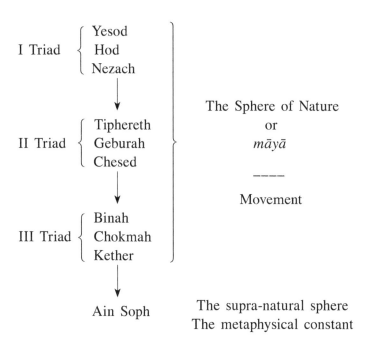

I Triad $\left\{\begin{array}{l}\text{Yesod}\\ \text{Hod}\\ \text{Nezach}\end{array}\right.$

The Sphere of Nature
or
māyā

II Triad $\left\{\begin{array}{l}\text{Tiphereth}\\ \text{Geburah}\\ \text{Chesed}\end{array}\right.$

————

Movement

III Triad $\left\{\begin{array}{l}\text{Binah}\\ \text{Chokmah}\\ \text{Kether}\end{array}\right.$

Ain Soph   The supra-natural sphere
The metaphysical constant

The metaphysical sphere is that of Ain Soph, and it is toward it that the disciple who follows the "Pathway of Fire" must tend.

Although some triads may express exceptional and universal qualities, nonetheless they are operating in the dominion of "the natural", the objective, of duality (subject-object), of becoming and, therefore, of time, space and causality.

The middle course is "The Pathway of Fire" which from Malkuth leads to Tiphereth, Da'ath, Kether and, finally, to Non-Being as Absolute-Constant.

THE PATHWAY OF FIRE

30. We have spoken of the "Pathway of Fire" with reference to the *Qabbālāh*, the *Advaita Vedānta* and the *Asparśa Yoga* and, although our readers have already understood its meaning, we feel it is nonetheless important to clarify its significance.

The "Pathway of Fire" has, obviously, nothing to do with the element of fire proper; it indicates the "Way" (*sādhanā*) along which to travel in order to realize one's own Essence. Even in *Yoga* terms one may say that the *kundālinī* fire which resides at the base of the spinal chord, must join with the fire of *Śiva* which is at the top of the head. It is, therefore, an experiential, operative and realizative way.

We might also use the expression "The Pathway of Sound" (*śabdamārga*) because sound too is subject to manifestation and the disciple realizes himself as Sound and finally as non-sound Essence. Aum is the primordial sound, the vibrating dart; even Light is primordial Fire. Thus one may speak of luminous Sound and of resounding Light or Fire. In Sanskrit "sound" is called *svara* and "light" *svar*; sound and light are thus united by their essential phonetic affinity. On the basis of this identity between light and sound, in the *Ṛg Veda* the Cantor is called the *svabhānavah*, that is, "he who is self-luminous".

According to the *Qabbālāh* the Light-Word emerged from the depths of Darkness. Therefore the "Pathway of Fire" is the *path* that every disciple must travel along whatever Branch of

Tradition he chooses. This is the Way of "Return". As a result, it is neither a particular or individual teaching, nor again, a collateral way with respect to the sole and only main Way. In truth such an expression sprang up innocently yet appropriately. He who is writing, having received the *Asparśa* and *Vedānta Advaita* teaching, at a certain point during his *sādhanā* was told to light the Fire, to burn himself with the Fire and to dissolve himself in Fire. This "Way" is also related to the God Agni, considered in the *Veda* as the Lord of the triple world. But Agni also represents the flame of aspiration toward the most High, which in the end fills the heart with the devouring Fire of pure Consciousness. (It is obvious that certain suggestions can have a meaning only for he who receives them). Later, studying some of the other Branches of Tradition, the writer realized that, after all, each disciple, to whatever Branch he belongs, follows his "Pathway of Fire".

Now let us examine each sephirah in a detailed way, starting from the bottom.

YESOD

31. Yesod (foundation) is the foundation of and the substance from which all things at the objective level are made. It expresses the "lower Waters", while the symbol of the upper Waters is Binah. Between Yesod and Binah there exist, therefore, precise correspondences; on the one hand Binah, (primordial substance, equivalent to *Prakṛti* in *Vedānta*, the universal Mother-nature), stimulated by Chokmah-Kether, is the material cause of manifestation; on the other hand, Yesod (lower lunar nature-substance, more "material" and grosser) brings into objective manifestation (Malkuth) those imaginative

impressions revived from Hod-Nezach. In the microcosm of the human being, the reproductive organs correspond to Yesod. This fact illuminates the function of Yesod just as, at the highest level, it illuminated the condition of Binah, when considered as the universal Mother. In *Yoga* terms Yesod corresponds to *Prāṇa* (supra-physical element) and it is in the body-sheath *Prāṇamaya*, that the *cakra svādhiṣṭhāna*, the creator-center of the generating seed, exists.

Yesod is the quintessence of matter after the solid, liquid, gaseous and aeriform, or after the earth, water, air and fire elements. Therefore it is substance which goes beyond the sensorial-material plane because it is a supra-physical element. Every thing-event of the dense-physical dimension originates in Yesod; every correction, transformation or transmutation which is thought of at physical level must be prepared in Yesod.

Thus, every transformation which must be carried out in the cellular constitution of a human being must first occur in the gene which is the archetype-code of the physical cell. Therefore, Yesod is pre-material physical substance in which the archetypes produced by Hod converge and are made concrete and then later precipitated as prototypes in Malkuth. The true "operations" must be prepared in Yesod, not in Malkuth. The Yesod substance is plastic, mobile, fluid, sensitive to every kind of stimulus. As is well known, the electron is sensitive to the simple presence of an observer to such a degree that Heisenberg was inspired to formulate his theory of indetermination. But Yesod is sensitive above all to Hod, which represents the mind, another even more pliable, subtle, powerful and penetrating substance.

With reference to the sexual polarity, one must say that Yesod, being by nature the sphere that causes all objectivity, represents propulsion toward polar union with a view to generating and procreating. All sexual movements and impulses occur upon this level and avail themselves of the corresponding physical organs for fulfillment and precipitation. Hyper-stimulation in this sphere may lead to many conflicts and degeneration and, as a result, it is only by turning one's attention toward the causal sphere, and not toward the physical sphere, that one can solve these problems.

It is not upon the dense plane that one must operate to solve certain organic disharmonies, in this precise case the sexual ones, but upon the plane of Yesod, as second cause of disharmony-degeneration, and even more upon that of Hod-Nezach as the prime cause.

In conformity with the propelling power of Hod, the Yesod substance may crystallize an event-thing for such a long time as to render it inertial. From here stems what is generally known as a "subconscious content" of the instinctive-organic, material order.

Since the human being is a perfect copy of the macrocosm and synthesizing within himself the totality of life, it possesses window-centers which open upon the various existential planes. Generally these window-centers are closed (only the one on the dense physical plane is open), wherefore one is unable to either see or operate on the various levels of life, but with a certain degree of "sensitivity", they can often be perceived.

There are two ways in which, in general, one can come into contact with the world of the Powers:

1) By opening these window-centers and thus, in perfect awareness, *being* and operating upon the various planes.

2) By means of rite, and in this case one performs Theurgy. It is preferable to leave aside what is today commonly called "magic".

HOD

32. We stated above that Yesod is sensitive to the influence of Hod, rather, that its activity is determined by Hod itself. Hod is the positive-active agent and Yesod is the negative-passive one; when they are joined together the precipitation of Malkuth takes place. In other words, when the idea meets the formative plastic substance, expression upon the objective plane is achieved; or, when a thought meets the vocal cords – which are nervous fibers – words or sounds expressing that thought are produced. An idea that does not become "flesh" represents a phenomenon of vain sterility and pure onanism that may prove harmful to the creator himself.

Hod is even more vibrant and rarefied mercurial substance than that of Yesod, and its offspring is called idea. An archetypical form of Yesod, not nourished by Hod is a body without a soul; one might say that it is a miscarriage. The archetypical images of Hod are the energy vectors that mould the prānic-ethereal substance of Yesod. Hod does not act directly upon Malkuth, but upon Yesod. Hod is, therefore, creative thinking; in Hod the idea is *contemplated*, in Yesod the *support* and the suitable framework are created, in Malkuth the idea is *expressed* and materialized.

Thus one obtains a threefold expressivity that represents the creative modality of Gods and men. This triplicity includes the spirit, the soul and the body. The spirit is the nucleus-essence or the noumenon; it is the Entity, regardless of the nature, the dimension or the level it may belong to; the soul is the formative *water*, the plastic mediator, the placenta that nourishes the nucleus bringing it to maturity; the body is the vehicle of the nucleus-entity's objective expression.

The true *demiurge* operates above all in the sphere of Hod; according to its "contemplative power", Yesod automatically moulds itself causing the seed of contemplation to precipitate into Malkuth. A *demiurge* is not very interested in the raw material as he sees to it that the plastic mediator models itself appropriately on the propelling force of the contemplative act alone.

33. Hod is essential noumenal or principle/substance (with regard to the individualized psychic triad), but it receives the impulse of life from the sphere of Nezach. Hod becomes passive and negative toward Nezach while toward Yesod, as we have seen, it is active and positive.

Nezach represents the original impulse to manifest love for life and living (its lower octave is represented by desire). It is the prime force of descent, externalization and precipitation. Without this vital impulse, Hod would not have the opportunity to organize himself as a nucleus, nor would Yesod as a plastic mediator, nor, as a result would there be forms upon the physical-objective plane. Nezach is the force of nature that urges Hod *to formulate*. Its upper-middle octave is Chesed and its universal supreme octave is Chokmah. Just as at strictly *objective* level without desire one cannot obtain any formative effect, so also without Nezach's willpower there is no impulse to think either; we mean "to think" and not to be thought; the majority are passive objects of thought disorder, which is why they do *not create*.

In Nezach the love-life-impulse proceeds toward the external; in Hod this impulse actualizes as noumenon whereas in Yesod it finds its animating food, and in Malkuth it becomes manifest and appears.

From this point of view we thus have a complete triad as well as a plane of precipitation.

Nezach = generating life – Venus
Hod   = nucleus – emerging quality – Mercury
Yesod   = molded archetype – Moon.

NEZACH

34. Nezach means "victory" or "firmness" because it is the victorious and firm impulse which generates and determines upon the plane of Hod. One may also point out the following correspondences: Nezach is the inspirer, Hod the thinker and composer, and Yesod the moulder; Nezach intuits and wills, Hod geometrizes and Yesod animates and precipitates.

Without the propelling power of Nezach, Hod would remain sterile and, in turn, without the thinking impulse of Hod, Yesod remains still and in latency. The mind of itself does not confer any power; if, however, it is electrified by the incisive and directional *potency* of Nezach, then it becomes a "tension field" ready to coagulate a *nucleus-being*.

Nezach, Hod, Yesod and Malkuth form the lower quaternary because they refer, as far as the human being is concerned, to individuality. In fact, individuality is composed by these sephiroth which, badly directed, create the urge to be selfish, to split and differentiate. Thus, the life impulse of Nezach may be directed toward individualization. What is called psychic world is composed of these three sephiroth (while Malkuth represents the physical element); it is the world of shadows. If one keeps in mind that the majority, in time-space, through the power of Hod, have created indefinite form-images which dwell in the subtle sphere, then one can understand why it is so difficult to perceive the True, the Just and the Beautiful.

By means of his mental mercurial power, man created many psychic monsters which, as they were nourished more and more, superimposed themselves upon the true archetypes of the plane of Briah. One of these monsters is the empirical ego. This is a psychic compound with which the consciousness identifies. Ninety per cent of magical ability, spiritism, pseudo intuitions, the power of mediums, reception of sounds and light, etc., derive from these image-forms belonging to the psychic order. They are so alive, so pulsating and so concrete as to fool even the expert. The appearance of Entities such as Christ, Buddha and others belongs to this intermediate psychic world. Many spiritual and occultist texts come from *ghosts* belonging to the Hod-manasic (*manas* = mind) world. At times they are harmless "inspirations", other times they are inspirations that create confusion and distortion of truth, sometimes they are evil and bring with them conflicts, deviations and false truths concerning all the fields of human life, thus leading men down a "blind alley". Anti-traditional forces operate in this ghostly sphere created by irresponsibility and individual ignorance. When it is not placed under the power Tiphereth, the sphere of individuality works for the individual and particular, for self-assertion and thirst for acquisitions and enjoyments, its action aims at compensating for the lack of wholeness, which can be found, instead, in its transcendental state.

The human being is universal and if he seeks to circumscribe and limit himself he cannot but degenerate and perish. He is not only Nezach, Hod, Yesod and Malkuth, he is also Tiphereth, Chesed and Geburah; in fact, he is much more. If his direction is not upward, toward a completion of himself, toward the awakening of his whole nature, he will find himself traveling the road of *saṁsāra*, of conflictual becoming and compensation. Individuality *creates* all things in this world of ghosts *to compensate* for its impotence and its restlessness. Those who operate magically and only in this sphere contribute toward the creation of disorder and greater suffering.

Sexual magic (Yesod), ritualistic and imaginative magic (Hod), divorced from the directing principle of Tiphereth lead to a blind alley and to the world of Qelippoth, that is a world of darkness, disharmony and imbalance. One-sidedness, fanaticism, selfishness, etc. are imbalanced effects of universal harmonic Reality.

IDEA-NUMBER-NAME

35. Sephirah means "number" because it represents a certain degree or a harmonic of the Kether-note; it also contains what the *Qabbālāh* calls Idea and Name.

Universal unfolding and re-absorption are reproduced in a *numerical scheme* which reflects in its combinations the weave and the architecture of the cosmic building and fixes its various stages.

The Name is the Word of Power, the Word which the Primordial Kether, the noumenal One, the fundamental Sound, assumes upon that certain plane of existence. To pronounce the Name of a particular sephirothic sphere means making it vibrate; it is like sounding the key of a piano, it means setting in motion the Intelligence that governs that sphere. The existential totality of an entity is enclosed in a Name and this is equivalent to luminous Sound.

The Idea is an Intelligence, a Power, a Principle, a Law acting in life, a universal Center of "personalized" action. It is the Name which has individualized itself, which has taken on a precise configuration.

Thus we have ten Names which are the sub-sounds of the sole divine Name-sound, and ten Intelligences-Powers each with a law-giving task to perform.

If the Name is the cause of *movement* on a plane, the Idea-Intelligence is its direction, its development, the principle that governs that plane.

With reference to the sephirothic triad which we spoke of above, the Name of Yesod's numeration is *Shaddai* (omnipotent), the Idea-Intelligence is the Archangel *Gabriel* (man of God) who is the head of the angelic host of the *Cherubim* (the Strong); every time, therefore, one invokes these angelic hosts – which are particular vibrations producing certain effects – they answer.

Hod's sephirah-numeration has the Name of *Elohim Shabaoth* (God of the armies), while its Idea-Intelligence is *Michael* (God-like) who is the leader of the angels *Ben Elohim* (Sons of God).

Nezach's sephirah-numeration has the Name of *Tetragrammaton Shabaoth* or *Adonai Shabaoth* (God of the Hosts), while his Idea-Intelligence is called *Haniel* (grace of God) who is the leader of the angels *Elohim* (Gods).

We should consider that in the *Haṁsa Upaniṣad*, which is a part of the *Yoga Upaniṣad*, the pathway of *Brahman* consists in the gradual recognition of ten sounds. At a certain point the *Upaniṣad* proposes: «We must transcend the first nine sounds and concentrate our attention upon the tenth which is that of thunder... he becomes *Brahman* at the tenth, realizing union of the soul with *Brahman*». This *Upaniṣad*, as one can well see, is of the metaphysical order because it transcends the nine sounds that represent the world of *māyā* or "nature". In cabalistic terms one might say: one must transcend the nine sephiroth and resolve oneself in Kether. This is the middle Way, the Pathway of Fire, the metaphysical Way, that of initiation, which is for that human being who has awoken to the consciousness of transcendent being.

36. The name and the form taken in themselves, have no value. The name is nothing but a denomination of a Strength, an Energy, of an underlying reality. For example, one attributes the *name* of "electron" to a certain energy-reality. The name separated from the named reality is pure nothing. Thus a form (an image, a figure, a face, an effigy) is a configuration, a representation, an aspect of reality. If, after all, the name and the form are simple *mental representations*, what they represent is, on the contrary, real.

To call a certain thing by its proper *name* means to *stimulate* it, render it active and responsive. Thus to call an individual by his proper name means giving him the possibility of *answering*. From this point of view we may speak of *Invocation*, which in turn causes *Evocation*. These terms must be taken in a very special sense, not in the sense that is normally attributed to them. Whoever understands the "law" of Invocation and of Evocation is capable of "dialoguing" with Life.

It is obvious that if we apply this to the case of the single human being, to evoke in him a response we must only call him by his name uttering his name verbally, using the voice, vocal sound, because this is the way in which he can receive an invocation. This implies that every level, every sphere of life or every existential plane expresses itself using its own language (sound) and its own form (color).

For example, were he who desires to invoke Kether to go to the window and simply call out his name, he might well wait for years, for cosmic cycles, without receiving any response.

What we wish to describe is something that genetically precedes any formulated name and all logically based conceptual expressions. It is something primordial and supra-conceptual and therefore has no bearing upon intellective comprehension. The Ancient Egyptians called this indefinable aspect of the name-sound a "cry" of the God Toth. The *Haṁsa Upaniṣad* speaks of "thunder".

When we evoke within ourselves a name or a word, we can notice – if we feel sensitive toward that word – that, like the echo of a trumpet or a bell, our being begins to vibrate and respond until it is completely taken, exalted, at times even enraptured (*samādhi*).

More than of Word we should speak of "resounding Syllable"; or, rather, of "vibrating Monosyllable" because it evokes that "cry" or that primordial supra-conceptual sound which gave origin to manifestation.

The *Aitareya Upaniṣad* (I, 4) includes the primordial Sound in the cosmic Egg: «(*Puruṣa*) hatched it. And, having hatched it, his mouth opened wide like an egg. From his mouth came the *word*, from the word the *fire*»: therefore, sound and light or, as we said above, luminous sound and resonant light-fire.

Sound is the vehicle of creation or of destruction whereas the name, that is the particular resonant combination, represent its seal and its symbol. Thus, to pronounce that name means to cause all vital things that depend upon it to vibrate.

Let us recall the three data: Name, Idea, Number, or Sound, Quality, Number.

The resonant combination depends on the scale-number and the sound itself produces tones (ideas); Name, Idea, Number (sound-vibration, quality, number) are a threefold unity. As a result, one has the Sound that produces number and quality, or Number that produces sound and quality, etc.

Quality or tonal values are the subjective aspect, while number represents the objective datum.

«The wealth of *sāman* is its musical tone (*svara*)».

(*Bṛhadāraṇyaka Upaniṣad*: I, III, 25)

«Tao fills the whole universe... This essence may not be called up through noise, but through sounds».

(*Chuang-tzè*: XVI, 1)

A sephirah-Number constitutes an objective element of the Idea-Intelligence which presides over a particular existential plane. The Name is the *Harmonic* of the primordial Note (Kether). To receive the quality-idea it is necessary to re-educate one's inner string or *sensitivity* of consciousness (a condition that goes beyond mere psychic sensitivity, which is simple animal *reaction*), so as to be able to attune oneself to the quality-sound-fire of a sephirah.

If one proceeds along the central *string* of the Tree (Pathway of Fire) one has the possibility of perceiving and grasping the luminous resonant quality within oneself (*to be* Idea, to live sephirothic Harmony), while if one operates upon the lateral *strings* one obtains, above all, number-sound (rite). In that case one must pay great attention because the inner string of the operator's consciousness, not being related with the qualitative power of the entity evoked, may break. Man always operates outside of himself, he is always the executor of ritual actions, be he a scientist, a magician, a philosopher or a musician, but Reality is within oneself and, in order to be able *to grasp* and *evaluate* life-reality, one must live it, that is, *vibrate* it; one must *be*. The expressive Quality of life may be vibrated and experienced by an appropriately trained *consciousness string*.

It is necessary to reflect on the fact that the *Qabbālāh* is not a set of formulae for playing cards, or a book for calling up the "dead", or a recipe-book of magic for prestidigitators, or a form of religious mysticism as is normally meant by this term.

The *Qabbālāh* is a traditional Science and Metaphysical discipline, therefore, it acts within the Greater and the Lesser Mysteries, it is *apara* and *parāvidyā*.

As the science of Invocation-Evocation is of a specific vibratory order and right position of consciousness, and since it requires right rhythm, it cannot be taught to all. It implies adequate qualification because it is also the fruit of intuition.

Thus, one must not put oneself "before" the Law-Strength, but *be* that Law-Strength; incarnate, incorporate and annex that Strength, especially if one touches the world of Principles without form.

The human being is a center of resonance: he is capable of receiving and transmitting the Word, he is a *vessel* that may be filled and pour forth, and does not require a material Temple in order to act and *attract* the Intelligences. because he himself is a Temple, the living symbol by which the Idea reveals itself.

37. Therefore, one must distinguish between *Realizing* a Power, until one is *unity* with It, and putting oneself upon the plane of magical and objectified dualism.

Doubtless, the first method implies transfiguration of oneself, accord with oneself and comprehension of oneself; it means revolutionizing one's own incompleteness and limitedness and transcending the formal; while the second implies only empirical practice and training.

The majority prefer ceremonial magic of the formal order because they do not wish to transform themselves or work upon themselves, but simply to gather up crumbs of curiosity, of insignificant information concerning this or that, or to utilize energies to dominate the weak and the ignorant, or tricks to baffle the ingenuous.

The sephirothic Tree does not represent an operative means by which to win for oneself the sympathies of some sephirah or other, but the Path of Fire, in order to be Gods rather than men, a Path to unveil Kether and, for those who are prepared for it, to integrate with Ain Soph Aur.

38. It is worthwhile saying again that the human being is a being to the image and likeness of Kether and has in himself the vibratory wholeness that exists in the entire cosmos. His intention must be that of *vibrating* within himself those chords capable of making him attune to the universal Intelligences. In this way he universalizes himself and becomes co-participant of the existing Whole.

When, for example, he *vibrates* Love, man is "in tune" with Tiphereth-Chesed. We insist upon the concept of *vibrating with* and not simple utterance of (using the vocal cords) the name of the sephirah or the Intelligence – with regard to this point we think we have been quite clear.

If the universe is upheld by vibratory Entities which express *qualities* and therefore influences, by evoking within ourselves those qualities we can relate to certain Entities. If, wishing to evoke the central Chesed-Geburah-Tiphereth triad, we vibrate within ourselves hatred and separateness, we run the risk of attracting the *influences* of Qelippoth, rather than those of the desired triad.

The cabalistic universe is composed of ten musical strings that resound with certain qualities which in turn emit specific influences. The individual, in his totality, possesses these string-windows and if he is able to re-sound them he enters into contact with the universal symphony.

The disciple who pursues the "Pathway of Fire", therefore the operative or realizative Way, must know how to find within himself the right notes capable of enabling him to belong to the universal confraternity of the Harmony of the spheres.

Normally a human being expresses qualities that attune him to the unbalanced aspects of the sephiroth. The task of the Tree is to stimulate the Consciousness to express Accord, Harmony and Unity of life, and have those who are prepared transcend completely the world of vital *qualities* itself (pure metaphysical Pathway). To implement all this one must consider that the lower triad receives its raison d'être from the middle triad and seeking to cut the former off from the latter means transforming individuality into an absolute entity, devoid of soul and spirit.

Thus, if one wishes that Nezach, Hod and Yesod achieve harmony with universal Life, that the microcosm be attuned to the macrocosm, then one must place the emphasis upon the Tiphereth note. This implies realizing a way which is no longer downward but upward; it means raising the tones; it requires transcending simple individuality and specific parts, and subjecting oneself to the Principle; that Principle which is the effective Center of a being as person.

To have an idea of what this means we may take a look at the following set of triangulations :

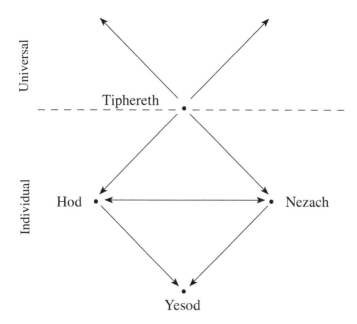

From this table we can deduce that:

a) The lower triad is the symbol of the upper one.

b) Yesod is the creative center of the lower triad and Tiphereth is the creative center of the upper triad.

c) Hod, Nezach and Yesod are the channels through which individualized consciousness can express itself. Tiphereth, with Geburah and Chesed, is the channel of universal consciousness.

d) The passage from the individual to the universal occurs following the destruction of the ego or egoistic level. This implies undertaking Initiation, real Initiation, because all those that are usually given objectively are merely symbolical.

e) The individual operates through instinct (Yesod), feeling (Nezach) and imaginative mind (Hod); the universal operates through light-intuition (Tiphereth), love-harmony (Chesed) and will-power (Geburah).

39. The path or way which leads from Yesod to Tiphereth is the 25th, called the Intelligence of temptation or Pathway of the trials.

The "Pathways of Wisdom" are the luminous roads along which men may arrive at the hidden Centers. There are 32 of these.

40. The *cakras* corresponding to the sephiroth in question are:

CAKRA	SEPHIRAH	PHYSICAL ORGAN
Svādhiṣṭhāna	Yesod	Generation
Viśuddha	Hod	Larynx
Maṇipura	Nezach	Solar plexus
Anāhata	Tiphereth	Thymus-heart.

41. To implement the process of reorientation and of solution of the energies one may follow three kinds of ascesis which rest – according to the case – upon Willpower, Harmony-Beauty and Knowledge (the central triad).

It is obvious that such a process of death-rebirth must be guided by an expert cabbalist who has been initiated into Tiphereth and who, finding himself consciously on the supra-individual plane, may as a result lead others into the universal.

There are people who know how to will, understand or feel the rhythm and beauty everywhere.

By means of Willpower one may achieve understanding and grasp Harmony-Beauty, or by means of Harmony-Beauty one may discover Comprehension and Will-justice-equilibrium; and, again, through Comprehension one may discover Harmony-Beauty and universal Willpower.

Comprehension devoid of Harmony-Beauty and of equilibrium or universal justice remains unbalanced. In actual fact, one may say that one has not attained Tiphereth; or, rather, by evoking Chesed, instead of passing through Tiphereth it passed through Nezach and then through Hod, creating in this way an unbalanced passion (Qelippoth). Religious fanaticism, which sometimes becomes criminal, stems from this kind of unbalancing of the individuality overstimulated by a superior power. This is also true of will (Geburah) that passes directly through Hod and not through Tiphereth.

If one is not careful and well guided in the evocation of the Intelligence-Powers, over-stimulations with consequent scission of individuality may occur.

Universal *dharma*-will is well explained in the *Bhagavadgītā*[1]. This will is, obviously, not of the individual, partial, sectarian kind; it is not even a type of willpower that can be associated with a particular realm of nature. All the kingdoms of nature express qualitative, universal archetypes and therefore the primordial Archetype.

The lower quaternary group separated from the intermediate triad can develop and even refine the various senses, so that *manas*-Hod may increase utilitarian intelligence, certain defense

---

[1] See, *Bhagavadgītā*, The Celestial Song, Translated from the Sanskrit and Commented by Raphael. Aurea Vidyā. New York.

mechanisms (and not only physical ones) as well as faculties for offense (even going as far as to invent very sophisticated means), but it cannot develop that sense of universality, of all-inclusiveness, of vertical spirituality which is capable of carrying out synthesis and unity of one's consciousness.

What is normally called "progress" is a kind of monstrous ability and an unbalanced intelligence both of which operate for the "preservation" of the ego, meant as body and as psyche. This supposed progress, in actual fact, obscures that "sensitivity" which leads to synthesis unity and the transcendent spirituality. Acquisitive and preserving intelligence which operates exclusively within the individual order does not allow the consciousness of "fallen" man to progress at all. So-called progress is nothing but a phenomenon of metallization, solidification or terrestrialization, that is to say, a limitation of awareness. The progress of an individual is determined insofar as he is able to fit into the context of universal harmony, to recognize himself as an active element or as a link in the cosmic chain of life, to discover that he is a brother among brothers, and not only within the ambit or modality of the human life.

42. One thing must be taken into consideration: many believe that they are already integrated individuality, but this is not so. There are very few who truly will, think, feel and act.

The majority of individuals express certain "energies" and the center-consciousness automatically and impotently identifies with them. Thus, according to the energy of the moment – thought, emotion or instinct – they are compelled and conditioned. Their energy faculties are torn apart, separated and not coordinated by the center-consciousness. There are people who are compelled and conditioned by a certain line of thou-

ght, others by a certain emotional-sentimental direction, etc.,
without their knowing it. Besides, this disassociated wanting,
thinking and feeling enters into a relationship of "sympathy"
with the collective unconscious whereby a further reciprocal
conditioning is caused as well as interactions urging toward a
greater degree of automatism. When certain sephirothic Energies
are evoked then the question becomes even more complica-
ted, because as we said above, individualized energy currents
are over-stimulated and potentiated and at the same time not
integrated in the ego-conscience. Thus certain tendencies and
maniacal sexual obsessions with unilateral interpretations of
reality are unleashed; one may obtain a conceptual, sentimental
or sexual-instinctive accenting of reality. One may also, as often
happens, be obsessed by a will for power or, to put it more
appropriately, by a *desire* for power characterized by a need
to gratify the ego-center. There are "spiritualists" and even
"initiated" who have developed and potentiated the Hod-mind
and have been dragged – despite themselves – onto the plane of
criticism, opposition, dogmatic individualism, or of the "wise"
ones who aim at judging or demonstrating a point of view at
all costs; people like these may even transform themselves into
executioners, or fault-finders, into henchmen who take up the
vindictive hatchet instead of the scepter of imperturbability.
They use concepts magically in order to strike rather than to
reveal truth innocently; and all this while employing words such
as universality, comprehension, vital unity, reason, identity or
metaphysical reality. There are also "adepts" who speak in the
name of love, of brotherhood, etc., but with such a degree of
blindness as to be capable of awful revenge if someone dares
to oppose them. The former kind are more dangerous because
the magic powers of Hod have no limits, the *manas*-Hod may

be capable of anything as it creates formidable alibis against which very few can resist; upon the plane of the word all are right and all are able to find valid justifications and defenses. Outrages, absolutisms, envy, acrimony, separation, revenge, crime and a thousand other things can all find a justification, only because the magical power of the conceptual imagination is put to the service of the egotistic monster.

Here we are undoubtedly within the realm of Qelippoth, of obsession, and of alteration of the proper Accord. When a strengthening of the ego itself (as directional synthesis of the faculties), rather than of single factors or of particular psychic powers, occurs, then the danger is even greater; it is so great, in fact, that we wish the history of men, which has known several such cases, may produce increasingly less of them.

43. Chesed, Geburah and Tiphereth, as we have seen, represent the central triad, the universal Soul, the intermediary between the objective and the integrally subjective. If one may compare deep night to the primordial or principial triad and day to the material triad, the idea of dawn may be connected with the central triad.

The lower triad individualizes because it is of the selective order, the central triad universalizes because it is of the synthetic order; the former operates principally upon the plane of "dispersion", the latter upon that of "cohesion" and union.

These terms are simply symbols which express peculiar energies or Intelligences. In the physical world we have energies that express cohesion, fusion or fission and energies that express dispersion, break-up or scission; these forces are the effects of causes that originate from the central triad. As long as these forces are balanced there is life and harmony; when, due to certain circumstances, they become unbalanced, there is death and disharmony.

In relation to its planets, the sun acts as a bipolar force of attraction and repulsion at the same time. If this force were to become unbalanced or disharmonious, this would lead inevitably to the death of the planets because they would either be attracted and completely "absorbed" by the sun, or thrust off, hurled away out into the interstellar space. The same is true of the physical atom: if its cohesive-repulsive balance did not function harmoniously it would die.

Chesed-Geburah is a bipolar, cohesive-repulsive Intelligence-energy and has its point of harmonic expression in Tiphereth. If the individualized consciousness of the lower triad fails to respond to the harmonic rhythm of Tiphereth, it breaks up and splits until it is scattered in a chaotic manner. To make a correlation, it is the Tower of Babel. (At present on planet Earth, and on the human level, there are two political-social forces at work; the one is individual and selective, the other cohesive, communitarian and collectivistic, but they are in opposition, they strive one against the other, besides both being exclusive and rigid. If one could find the point of union, which obviously transcends the materialistic conception of the one force and of the other, humanity might well be able to march toward a fruitful period of harmonic and stable interrelations. By meditating upon the sephirothic Tree in full depth we can also find explanations to specific human problems).

If the lower triad wishes to operate harmonically it must raise its eyes up to the sky and follow the "way of Tao", the way of heavenly Harmony, the way of Beauty-order, the way of universal Fire. The earthly Jerusalem must conform to the Heavenly one.

The Tiphereth-Initiated lives in this Jerusalem or in Beauty-order, because he has made himself subject to it, having restored his cohesive-selective Powers to the proper archetypical rhythm.

The Tiphereth-Consciousness revealed by the greatest *Avatāras* has brought cohesive-selective energy onto the physical plane.

Jesus said that, besides universal Love, he had also brought the sword. *Śaṅkara* brought cohesive and unifying Knowledge but also revolution, the same is true of Buddha; but their actions were in harmony with the universal Order, while in many of their followers there was more selective, dispersing, individual and, at times, oppressive energy (unbalanced Geburah).

44. It is advisable to remember that to evoke the sephiroth Chesed or Geburah without first harmonizing one's own individualized energies means overstimulating certain flows of energy which operate within our psycho-physical spatiality; this means heading, without realizing it, toward the realm of Qelippoth; it is in this way that we are enslaved by maniacal-sexual, passionate-sentimental or conceptual-representative expressive one-sidedness.

We wish to insist once more upon the fact that the immediate goal of the cabalistic disciple is the evocation of the Tiphereth sephirah and of the Raphael Intelligence which presides over that sephirah.

Tiphereth expresses Beauty which is order, eurhythmics and sacrifice because it donates itself, offers and concedes itself so that the "darkness may be illuminated". Tiphereth is dominated by the sun and represents the first major Initiation; with the eye of Tiphereth one sees universe-life in terms of Harmony, Accord, Order and Comprehension. It also represents the cosmic Christ-love, the Master of Life, the central Heart, the reflected Sun of its upper Pole, Kether. Tiphereth is the son of Kether upon a particular existential plane, just as the terrestrial Christ is the son of the heavenly Father.

45. As has been said earlier, there are many who instead of reaching Tiphereth, amuse themselves with manipulating strictly individualized energies to profane, utilitarian and en-

slaving ends; but one must also say that there are many who, having reached maturity, and having challenged the "powers" of certain inferior material spheres, know how to take flight toward the majestic peaks of Wholeness and Fullness.

46. Kether is the One in which all Is, from which all proceeds and to which all returns. Da'ath is the First-born which operates upon non-formal levels, it is the universal Mind (*Mahat*); Tiphereth is the second born which operates upon formal levels. "Whoever sees Me, sees the Father": this is the consciousness of Tiphereth. This sephirah is a ray of light from Kether offered to formal-objective beings who live in the darkness of individuality, so that they may be able to find the Way of Beauty, Justice and Goodness. Tiphereth is the universal Christ given as a gift to the offspring of men so that they may become sons of God.

The salvation of conflictual, unilateral and passionate beings resides, therefore, in Tiphereth, because it is the central, mediating and unifying sephirah; it is the true heart of Kether, the heart which unites and fuses within itself the upper and the lower, the right-hand and the left-hand sides of the Tree. Tiphereth is considered as being the Small Face because it synthesizes the six sephiroth of the universal Edifice.

KETHER-CHOKMAH-BINAH

47. Because it stands above all the others, the first sephi-rah is called the Crown, the Old Man, the Primordial or the smoothed Point («When the *Setīma dekol setīmīm*, mystery of mysteries, decided to unveil itself, it determined first of all a sole Point; initially the Infinite was completely unknown and did not give off any light before the manifestation of this Point of Fire»), the white Head or the long Face. It contains all the other sephiroth and it unveiled them in the following order: the masculine, active or positive sephirah called Chokmah and its opposite, negative, passive, feminine polarity called Binah. These two poles, also called *'Abbā* (father) and *'Immā* (mother) produced the unifying power called Da'ath (omniscience) which remained hidden, veiled or esoteric because it is to be found upon the non-formal plane of the principle. The triad (Chokmah-Binah-Da'ath) caused the polarity Chesed (masculine, positive, active) and Geburah or Din (feminine, negative, passive); in turn this polarity produced the unifying power of Tiphereth.

This unifying Intelligence gave rise to masculine, positi-ve, active Nezach and its opposite, feminine, negative, passive pole, Hod. This polarity produced the unifying power of Yesod which, in turn precipitated Malkuth, also called *Shekīnāh*, upon the plane of objectivity.

48. The initial or principial triad – Kether, Chokmah and
Binah – expresses the primordial diffusive aspect; it represents
the seed of universal Life at the as yet non-manifest state.

It is the prime Cause (while the central triad is the second
cause of objective life), it is the noumenon of the manifest and
non-manifest whole.

«In Him (Kether) all is right hand» because the left is
turned toward the Infinite, Ain Soph.

Kether is also considered as the supreme Crown, the central Point of the circle, the Ancient of the days, the Amen,
the inscrutable Height and the Aum. His Name is 'Ehjeh (=
I am); and his Idea-Intelligence is called *Metatron*. He is the
God-Person adored by mystics and by the religious in general. In reality he is not a person in the everyday sense; man
anthropomorphizes the very Principles themselves. Kether is
existential essence, pure Being from which all springs; it is
certainty of the unity of life surpassing all possible duality
and fragmentation. In the eye of Kether what for us is multiplicity appears as undivided unity. Multiplicity is nothing but
appearance or visual distortion which is unable to embrace
micro and macrocosmic, individual and universal, formal and
non-formal unity-synthesis.

Kether, seen from the point of view of the individual is
both immanent and transcendent, inside and outside, but from
its own standpoint it is neither the one nor the other because it
transcends all dualism invented by Hod-Nezach; It is the Crown
which is set above the head because it includes all existence;

It is above the Universal Man or Adam Kadmon, above the manifest Intelligences themselves: Will, Love, Knowledge.

Whoever shall approach Kether shall approach the death of all formal and qualitative condition, however much his Essence may be "substantiated" with form and quality.

Kether is on the central pillar of the Arrow and also Meekness or equilibrium and its experience, if we can speak of experience, is that of Union; or better still, of Identity.

The true white Magician is one who, before every operation, becomes harmonized with the Kether-Metatron Power (and, obviously not only in words). The true cabalistic Magician is one who has laid down every burden and every vessel to allow divine Love-harmony to flow through his "instrument of contact".

We have mentioned that the Kether experience is identity with the Essence, which implies being beyond every evocation, all energy, the world of the Intelligences and beyond Theurgy and all that which implies duality and gross or subtle form. The realization of Kether passes through the *via negationis* or, rather, through the solution of both the lower and intermediate triad.

49. Kether, the One, the primordial Point is polarized in Chokmah and Binah, forming a threefold Unity. The two points at the base of the triangle are, therefore, the polarization of the point at the apex.

The sephirah Chokmah represents supreme Wisdom, the fruit-bearing Ray of primordial Light (Father) which is the cause of the fertility of Binah (Mother).

His Name is *JeHoVaH*. His Intelligence-Idea is *Raziel*.

«I (Chokmah-Wisdom) love those who love me and whosoever seeks me will find me...

God created me right from the beginning of his acts, even before his works...

The abyss did not as yet exist: I was conceived when the founts did not as yet gush forth...

When he fixed the skies I was present, when he drew a circle upon the face of the abyss...

... whoever finds me finds life and obtains the favor of the Lord; he who loses me wounds himself; and he who hates me has chosen death».

(Proverbs, VIII, 17, 22, 24, 27, 35)

The sephirah Binah represents the molding, creating primeval Intelligence. Its Name is *Jehovah Elohim*, its Idea-intelligence is *Tzaphkiel*.

POLARITY

50. It has been said that Chokmah represents the supreme Father (*'Abbā*), the stimulator of the universe, and Binah the Mother (*'Immā*; Marah = the Great Sea); one may express oneself in other terms and consider Chokmah as Essence and Binah as Substance, or Chokmah as a Ray of white primordial light and Binah as the instrument through which the prism of colors appears. Binah is the Great Sea, the primordial Waters, the receptive and generating darkness of the Abyss. They may be compared also to *Puruṣa* and *Prakṛti* of *Sāṁkhya* or *Viṣṇu* and *Brahmā* of *Vedānta*.

On the level of human physiology they represent the male spermatozoon and the female ovum; their encounter causes a third factor which is the Son of polar Union. The Son is the fruit of unitive Bliss (*ānanda*, love).

The Intelligences, the universal forms belonging to every order and level, are the daughters of *'Abbā-'Immā*.

Binah, as the creating material cause of the world of names and forms, is also destructive; in Binah forms are born and in Binah they grow and die; from this point of view its image is Severity (*Kālī*); in fact it constitutes the start of the left-hand lateral Pillar called, precisely, the Pillar of Severity, while Chokmah is the start of the Pillar of Clemency-Benignity.

Pay attention, however, not to attribute to these two terms (Severity-Benignity) their ordinary psychological, moral and individual connotations.

"Forms" are simply tools, instruments or cellular compounds by means of which Life circulates and Qualities unveil. Depending on the Qualities and Life, the forms turn, undergo variations and assume new expressions. For Chokmah-Binah they are a prestidigitator's "trick", "concrete movement", therefore *māyā*, to say it in *Vedānta* terms.

What appears cannot but disappear, what is born cannot but die; thus, the Giver of formal life cannot but be the Giver of death; but apparition and disappearance are tricks of illusion, simple fleeting phenomena which may be considered as dramatic events only by a consciousness that conceives them as absolutely real.

As we can see by examining the symbol on the facing page, the progression of the various sub-polarities occurs according to a specific order.

The study and the comprehension of these polarities (and of their points of synthesis) in all their various configurations – of which the sexual polarity is simply one and the lowest – afford the key to the many doors (50 according to the *Qabbālāh*) leading to the many Pathways of wisdom, that is, to Liberation.

It is hardly necessary to say that the two terms: primordial ovum and spermatozoon represent a simple analogy and an exemplification of the ontological reality.

AIN-SOPH

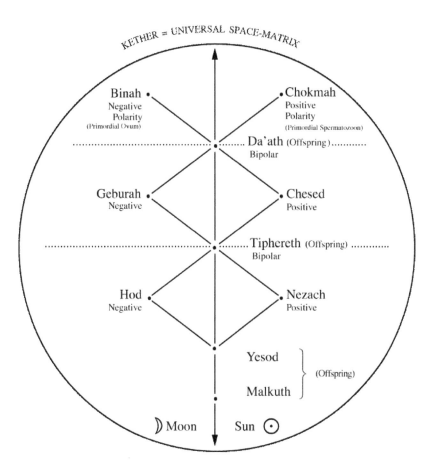

THE METAPHYSICAL PATHWAY

51. «The *Qabbālāh* describes the cosmogonical process in other ways too, for example by recurring to the image of the *Pargod* or the cosmic 'curtain'. The *Sohar* says that the 'Elder of elders' drew in front of Himself a curtain upon which an image of His kingdom appeared... We may say that the more God lowers his 'curtain' before Him the more He retreats into himself. The curtain rises before Him like a darkness which identifies itself essentially with his cosmic receptivity in which His infinite light is interrupted or stopped, as it were, by a veil, wherefore it appears only a distant and weak reflection of Him, like the 'vain' existence of all which is finite.

God is hidden in all that he creates, almost like the light in the innumerable sparkles of an enchanting mirage. The desert in which the mirage is formed is the symbol of the cosmic emptiness, or the 'place of the world' in God's bosom, created by *Zimzum* (contraction of divine luminous fullness), while the elusive screen upon which the illusory forms that fool the passerby are thrown is the symbol of the 'curtain' or of the 'mirror' of God, of his creative self-receptiveness, the *Shekīnāh*. Compared to the 'One without second', the entire creation with its archetypes – in that they are not absorbed by the sole Reality but emanate created things – assumes the illusory appearance of a 'second'. Therefore the *Qabbālāh*, in order to define the nature of the creation, accompanies the ideas of *Zimzum* and *Pargod* with that of vanity – illusion – or *Habel* derived from *Eccles*. 1, 2: "Vanity of vanities (*Habel habalim*)!... All is vanity (*Habel*)!". And the *Sohar* comments: "In this book king Solomon spoke of the seven vanities (*habalim*) upon which the world rests; they are the seven columns (the sephirothic columns of the Cosmic Edifice) which sustain the cosmos in its seven heavens (from which they are derived), *Vilon, Rakija, Shechakim, Sebul, Ma'on, Machon, Araboth* (as well as in their seven earthly effects or 'seven earths' and finally even their hellish darknesses or 'seven hells'). It is concerning these that Solomon exclaimed: "Vanity of vanities!... All is vanity!". There are seven heavens or firmaments and others (deeper existential planes) that (they too are divided into seven) derive from these and remain united with them, so that we have seven (fundamental) vanities and others that derive from them (all of which taken together form the 'great illusion' of the 'second'; in reality of the 'One without a second'). In his wisdom, Solomon spoke of these illusions (as well as of their archetypes and causes, that is of the seven sephiroth of the cosmic Edifice)»[1].

According to *Advaita Vedānta*:

«Certainly *māyā* has two powers: the projective one (*vikṣ epaśakti*) and the veiling one (*āvṛtiśakti*). From the subtle body to the gross one, all is created by the projective power»[22].

---

[1] Leo Schaya, *L'uomo e l'Assoluto secondo la Cabala*. Rusconi, Italy. (Italian Edition).

[2] *Dṛdṛśyaviveka*, Discernment between *ātman* and non-*ātman*: 13. Attributed to Śaṅkara. Translation from the Sanskrit and Commentary by Raphael. Aurea Vidyā. New York.

Pargod (curtain or cosmic veil) is equivalent to *āvṛtiśakti*, and *Zimzum* (limitation, contraction, projective concentration) to *vikṣepaśakti*.

The Tree or Cosmic Edifice, in its various dimensions and upon its various levels, seen from Ain Soph, is nothing but a simple projection or a weak reflection of the Reality without a second.

The ten sephiroth represent ideal "modifications" of Kether and even Kether is only a reflection of Ain Soph.

If we wish to give to the word Reality the meaning of Infinite, Uncaused, Constant, Absolute, outside of time-space-cause, then we can attribute it only to Ain Soph.

Kether is a simple spatial-temporal "harmonic" of the infinite possibilities of Ain Soph. Kether is the principial non-manifested Unmoved and the ten sephiroth are the movement; beyond motion and non-motion there exists Ain Soph, the Absolute without a second, the undifferentiated substratum from which objectified reflections depart and radiate.

If we find ourselves in the lower triad Nezach-Hod-Yesod, we are in the shade and in the realm of essentially fleeting phenomena; if we find ourselves within the central triad of Chesed-Geburah-Tiphereth then we are in the world of Ideas or Archetypes; if we find ourselves in the upper triad, that of Kether-Chokmah-Binah, then we are in the causal, generating world of the principle; and if, finally, we find ourselves in Ain Soph we are beyond shadows, Ideas and Principle, therefore, we are in the Infinite, in the one and only Reality, wherefore we have reached the deepest levels of *Pax profunda*, Bliss without object; we are in the Enchantment of the Unconditioned and Boundless.

The "Pathway of Fire" winds its way along the central pillar or line, it touches Malkuth, Yesod, Tiphereth, Da'ath, Kether and, in the end, Ain Soph. There are five centers that we must burn within our own psychic spatiality, five skeletons that we must reduce to ashes.

52. We said before that the Pathway which leads from Yesod to Tiphereth is the 25th, that of temptation or trials. This implies that, on our descent, the individualized world represents a strong temptation and a trial for the soul which sets out along this path.

Along the ascending line, to find oneself again in Tiphereth, one must:

a) resolve the crystallizations created by Hod; these are living form-images that dwell within the individual psychic spatiality and which makes life inertial;

b) stop the descending motion of energies, which implies making oneself the neutral center of the "ebb and tide" of energy;

c) re-orient the psychic movements in an upward direction, thus resolving the horizontal way of the individual; in other words, one must make a U-turn; this involves moving from an exteriorized state to an interiorized state.

This ascesis which requires *solution*, *fixation* and *re-orientation* cannot be described because it belongs to the particular subject who undertakes the ascesis. Each disciple has his own consciential state, his own *karma*, his own kind of energy, etc., and the ascent must be considered in connection with these data.

In any case it is possible to offer some brief explanations to those who are ready.

53. There is no *form* or *quality* that does not tend toward its own extinction, its own death, its own annulment.

Great efforts are made to perpetuate the world of forms and the qualities it expresses with a great waste of energy; and yet its end – despite all efforts to the contrary – is transformation (beyond form) and trans-quality (un-qualification).

In terms of physics, being is *form* (body-volume); in terms of psychology it is *quality* (psyche); in terms of theology and philosophy it is Consciousness-Life (Principle); in metaphysical terms it is One-without-a-second, absolute Constant, unqualified and uncaused Infinite.

Thus we have:

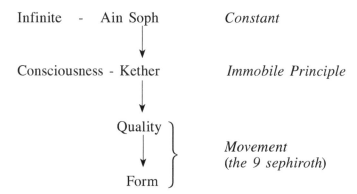

Infinite   -   Ain Soph   *Constant*

Consciousness - Kether   *Immobile Principle*

Quality
Form   *Movement*
                        (*the 9 sephiroth*)

We can *feel* the reactions of the form, we can *feel* the qualities from the form and we can *feel ourself* as being peaceful Life interwoven with Silence; Life which rests in itself and for itself.

When we have reached the great Silence, then the Consciousness, having resolved all motion, is attracted by Ain Soph.

54. One is the Consciousness, two is the quality, three is the form; the three are not separated but represent different modes of vital expression of the undivided Unity.

One is *Silence* (Kether), two is *movement* (Chesed-Geburah-Tiphereth), three is *prison* (Nezach-Hod-Yesod).

The "Pathway of Fire" consists in destroying the prison, resolving the movement and transcending the primordial Silence itself.

If one is *attracted* by Action or by Qualities (which give impulse to action) or by the principial Silence which resolves all and penetrates all, one is not ready to follow the "Pathway of Fire".

If one is *interred* in Action one is a slave of events, if one is urged by Qualities then one is a slave of enjoyment, if one is attracted by Silence one is a prisoner of *nirvāṇa*, Bliss or Paradise.

55. The way to Ain Soph is the way of *denial* (of appearances) and *affirmation* (of Ain Soph), it is a pathway of death and awakening, it is a pathway of solitude, courage and comprehension.

Many love to play with the Powers, a few love to dominate the Powers, very, very few love to transcend the Powers.

56. The lower triad is the flower, the intermediate triad is the stem, while the upper triad is the seed: the "Pathway of Fire" is the extinction or the solution of the *Seed*.

A Seed-principle is *one* of the *infinite* Seeds that Ain Soph may project upon its limitless screen. A Seed-principle, seen from the angle of Ain Soph, is *cause*, prison and conditioning.

The absolute Reality is more than a simple Seed-principle, however indefinite its vital expressions may be.

Whoever dwells in the Seed-principle dwells upon the plane of Necessity; whoever dwells in or, more appropriately, dissolves himself in Ain Soph, achieves total and absolute Freedom.

True Liberty is not freedom "to do", but it means being free "to do" or "not to do" – and this Liberty can be found only in the metaphysical dimension.

In the lower triad "doing" commands the individual; in the central triad the individual directs acting (and one cannot but act); in the upper triad we are in the realm of "non action"; only upon the plane of Ain Soph are we totally Free from the need to act or not to act.

57. In the lower triad we are governed by the Law, in the intermediate triad we are the Law, in the upper triad we are cause of the Law, while in Ain Soph one is above and beyond every Law; that is, one transcends the Laws of Being.

But, whoever is against the Law, outside of all Laws or violates the Law, is not in Ain Soph.

58. The mind, in its total extension may arrive at the prime Cause, but if it wishes to go further it must stop, because *That* (Ain Soph) cannot be a mentally perceived object but the fruit of *realization*.

The Infinite does not proceed from a *center,* from a *point,* because it is without center and without point, but it projects a center-point which is called Kether.

If the mind resolves itself in the center-point, it no longer produces "representative thought" because in the center-point both subject and object vanish.

If one "thinks oneself" as being center-unity one falls into a grave error, typical of minds that fail to grasp their own workings. The empirical mind can only *create an image* of the center-unity or Principial point; *to be* Point one must abandon volume, planes and lines, one must resolve oneself in Essence, one must not *think oneself* as center. Many believe or imagine themselves to be Silence, but *are not* Silence. Silence is the highest degree of realization upon the manifest plane.

One must distinguish between *imagining oneself* and *being.*

Every representation always refers to something, but Being does not refer to anything except to itself, insofar as it is pure Being.

Behind every representation there is He who represents, and when He who represents does not represent any longer there is Silence, Being or Consciousness without superimpositions or imaginings.

59. The imperfect and the perfect, the relative and the absolute, good and evil, lower and upper, etc., are representations of Hod which operates through "polar imagining".

It is not possible to imagine Ain Soph, it is only possible *to realize* It. It is easier to imagine than to realize, so there are many who imagine Kether, Chokmah and even Ain Soph.

Whoever follows the "Pathway of Fire" must abandon imagination, representations and conceptualizations; he must courageously die to all kinds of mental objectification. The only law one must follow is that which leads to Freedom.

On the Way of Return one must *extinguish oneself* in order to truly Be.

To quench the triple Fire (triple triad) one requires Maturity, Dignity, Daring and intuitive Knowledge.

Whoever has quenched the triple Fire – while still having a body – is a "living corpse" (*jīvanmukta* = living liberated one).

A "living corpse" leaves no tracks, has no *aims* to achieve or *duties* to fulfill.

The Fulfilled lives only in Fulfillment and Fullness, and this Fullness is free from all determinations, actions and purpose.

60. Tiphereth is universal comprehension, vital Harmony and also Knowledge, therefore, it assumes the role of Instructor but it must find the daring and determination to cross the Abyss and no longer dwell, even though not for individual reasons, in the world of "shadows".

Its flight toward Kether must be that of the swallow, without agitation or clamor; it must allow itself to be "attracted", it must glide without effort, without any resistance, into the One without motion.

During this flight that brings one higher and higher, and therefore toward the borders of the non-formal, one sees no "others"; words fail, thoughts cease, plans lose all meaning; there are no answers for anybody for, during this flight, the circumferences begin to fade, because one gradually discovers that nothing exists except the Self.

In the flash of the rays of the polar Sun the "shadows" become clear, become limpid and dissolve into points without dimension.

With whom can one speak if the "others" are not?

With what can one think if there is no projective mind and, therefore, no problems to solve?

To whom can one "cling" if there is no second as support?

The "Pathway of Fire" is the way without support, without relationship, because the ultimate Truth or Reality rests only upon itself. The "Pathway of Fire" is the Pathway of the Strong, of those who dare to plunge into the nameless Ocean, allowing themselves *to die* happily, to decompose, depolarize like a pinch of salt that dissolves in water.

61. One instant of distraction is sufficient to find oneself looking downward again: thus, the "shadows" reappear, they stand out against the horizon-screen and the *motion of relation* involves one once more.

Some seem to be *ready* but they lack decision; that decision which is not desire or aspiration; it is not even will, it is something that stems from the awareness that the existent All does not exist.

At certain levels, there are no techniques, philosophies, Gods to adore or energetic qualities to express. To "resolve oneself" one requires that Dignity and that Awareness which are consubstantial with the Being that has *comprehended*.

The Way of the Abyss is a Way of rediscovery, reintegration and unveiling of true, supreme and boundless Freedom.

62. Whoever loves Freedom (and certainly not that of the ego-shadow) has no choice but to pursue the way of the Ain Soph; the Abyss awaits those who love that Freedom which is peace and sweetness of fulfillment. That Abyss is capable of shattering the chains that for long ages have bound men in a dimension of identification and bewilderment.

A Pathway of Fire which is capable of extinguishing desire of power and existence (both individual and universal) awaits those who love Freedom; desire that, as a surrogate, tries desperately to compensate for that Freedom which is the fruit of neither human or divine projections.

Whosoever catches a glimpse of true Liberty can no longer allow himself to live in necessity, even if this belongs to the intermediate and upper triad.

Whoever loves absolute Freedom from all kinds of deceiving dualism can allow himself no weakness, hesitation, delays or alibis however noble and praiseworthy.

Whoever loves Freedom allows the triple world of necessity to burn itself out without regrets, lamentations or wonder: when the clear light of the sun shines on the horizon, who on earth would dare to cling to the weak, reflected light of the moon?

What we call life is in fact death, necessity and darkness; what we call death is Freedom and fullness of Being.

Binah is the creator of necessity but also of Freedom; if one is capable of daring, the destructive Fire of Binah may burn to ashes that life-death to which we cling so childishly on account of metaphysical ignorance.

If formal life is for the weak, to cling to the many bodily supports of life is also for the weak, and so is the urge to preserve; to die consciously is for the strong and they have the task of quenching the Fire that feeds *qualities* and *corporality*.

Tiphereth, Kether, Ain Soph: this is the Way of Fire. As humble reflection, Tiphereth must re-integrate with Kether; and as simple determination or Point of Ain Soph, Kether must *die* to itself and rediscover itself to be absolute Liberty.

63. At every level and degree, there are souls that descend, souls that keep what they have, and souls that lay down their *load* and, in courageous silence, choose the metaphysical Way of the unqualified Infinite.

If Ain Soph is the absolute Reality and Freedom without constraint, why therefore, should one fear? What can hold one back in the world of necessity?

There are souls that defend their own egoism, there are
souls that defend their own "mission", their own disinterested
action and their own *kṣatriya* (order of law-givers and rulers)
requests, and there are other souls that having transcended every
kind of doing and non-doing, action and non-action and, being
and non-being, dissolve themselves into metaphysical Silence.

The Way of the Abyss is the Way of Silence; but, beware,
noise might well re-attract you; those who were once our *fall*
shadow-companions might offer us stimulating sophisms and
cause us to fall again into imprisoning noise. One must be on
one's guard; what for some is nourishment is poison for others.

64. What we prospect here is the way to Ain Soph, not
to Yesod or Malkuth; we propose the way of "depolarization",
not that of "polarization"; we are pointing toward the way of
Re-integration not that of extroversion and generation.

If the iron compound (mass) wishes to dissolve into energy
it must attain silence and die to itself (as the element iron).

The Pathway of Return is the way of *solution*, *dispersion*
and *demagnetization*. The Pathway of Return is the way of
maturity, conversion and detachment. But it is not the way of
abandonment, flight or opposition. It is a good thing to reflect
upon this fact.

65. Knowledge is a thirst for Truth, love is a thirst for
Union-identity, will is a thirst for Being; Ain Soph is beyond
knowing, loving and willing.

66. We shall now re-propose what has been said about *Asparśa Yoga*[1], the pure metaphysical *Yoga*, because we feel that it is relevant to the pathway to Ain Soph.

«"The human being – says Meyerson – practices metaphysics just as easily as he breathes, without thinking about it.

The spontaneous need to transcend and create for oneself goals that are beyond one's own fleeting dimension is innate in human nature. Metaphysics was born with the cosmos itself because every particle of the universe tends toward its total existential reintegration.

The human being is a restless being, and has always been compelled to surpass himself, or rather to go beyond his own natural condition, to achieve a beyond that is often difficult to define but which, in actual fact, represents denial or refusal of all limitations and, therefore, of the finite composite world of appearances.

"The secret of the method – says Descartes – consists in seeking, with the utmost care, that which is most absolute" in everything.

The need of the Absolute is a primary necessity for man's mind, which implies that in all orders of reality there must be a Prime term (*ādi*) which is the condition of all the rest – and, as such, independent, at least within its own order – and which, in the strictest sense, may be considered as absolute, and as the only absolute without a second.

One should notice that that philosophy (especially modern and Western philosophy) which challenges man's capacity to

---

[1] See, Gauḍapāda, *Maṇḍūkyakarika*, The Metaphysical Path of Vedānta, Translation form the Sanskrit and Commentary by Raphael. Aurea Vidyā. New York.

discover the Absolute, merely transfers to the world of sensorial experience the character of absoluteness.

The metaphysician pursues the straight road of integral awareness and cognitive reintegration into the absolute Being from which all emanates and proceeds. More than taking an interest in the world of phenomena and structures, more than seeing how the "object-universe" is made, how its laws and its magical and deforming phenomena work, more than acquiring formal power, he directs himself toward the a-principial absolute Being or the Non-Being, toward the Undifferentiated, the Ineffable, the Unknowable (for the senses).

Metaphysics is interested in what is "beyond the physical", beyond nature, the gross and subtle forms, the substantial, the principial One itself and the God-Person; beyond all objectivity, subjectivity and all possible polarities. This implies that metaphysics deals with the Absolute, the Constant, the Infinite, Non-Being as pure and only Being, the Unconditioned, the One-without-a-second (*advaita*). Metaphysics thus goes beyond the physical, the psychic and the spiritual. All that which concerns the individual, and therefore the general, is to do with science; all that which concerns the universal, transcendental unity and totality, is to do with metaphysics.

If metaphysics is a quest for the Absolute or Reality without a second, then it cannot be schematized, conceptualized or placed within certain individualized mental frameworks. The Absolute or supreme Reality cannot be circumscribed, represented or brought upon the plane of empirical relativism, nor can it be considered the exclusive property of an individual or a people.

To achieve metaphysical Realization certain qualities are undoubtedly required – first of all, a mind capable of synthesis and of grasping the a-temporal. Most people are enslaved by time-space-causality and, in actual fact, it is very difficult to break free of it, but if one wishes to realize metaphysical knowledge one must *fly,* one must bring oneself beyond time and space, beyond the contingent, the individual and the general; in other words, one must learn to remain *without supports.* From this comes the name *aspar̄śa,* which means non-contact, without relations, rapport or support. Therefore one must also pay appropriate attention to this fact, because we are in the presence of a very particular and special type of knowledge which does not act according to the rules of ordinary discursive or empirical knowledge. This is the true 'Pathway of Fire' because at its touch all *māyā*'s objectifying possibilities are burned and because the entity reveals and shows itself in all its self-splendor. To grasp a-temporality in its immediacy means not to depend upon any empirical kind of *Yoga* practice or any type of psycho-physical exercise, it means suddenly immersing oneself in the all-inclusive and all-pervading Present. Metaphysical Realization can be implemented by means of that particular kind of mind which we might define as *mens informalis...*

The difficulty in grasping the absolute is great because it is not with the mind, which operates within the realm of subject-object, that one can comprehend non-duality. Vain are the efforts of those who try to consider the Absolute as a simple *object* of mental representation. One might say that *Aspar̄śayoga,* in order to be truly comprehended, necessarily and unequivocally imposes an Identity approach. In other words, being a *Yoga* without relationships, it is, obviously and above all, a *Yoga* without supports. Thus one must place oneself immediately within the Self, without leaning upon either external objects or qualifications of individuality such as feeling, willing or empirical knowing. The other types of

Yoga necessarily require aspiration, a vertical thrust and an impulse that nevertheless stem from individuality as the effect and aim at transcending individuality itself; these types of *Yoga*, therefore, require desire. Upon the pure metaphysical pathway it is no longer desire which determines what occurs, but awareness of "finding oneself", awareness of Being. The disciple is not pushed, he is held back; one might say that he is not compelled toward the acquisition of something, whether of the upper or the lower order, but toward the resolution of every request of *māyā*, including that of Union in the ordinary sense.

The disciple of *Asparśayoga* withdraws in himself and comprehends the Absolute, which unfolds in all its majesty within the secret recesses of his heart. Beyond all ideas, concepts, idols and phenomena, there is *That*, which is Totality, not subject to or dependent upon any concept or change. The 'metaphysically Reintegrated' have the privilege and the power to see all phenomena of life in the light of the metaphysical Zero.

Asparśayoga leads to liberation, or better still, to active reintegration (in actual fact one cannot speak even of liberation in the case of this type of *Yoga*) and realizes that sole, undifferentiated, uncreated or a-causal unmanifest and impersonal Essence from which the whole object-universe, as a chain of *māyā* perceptions of light, sprung. Being *is*, and one cannot add anything further, because to say that Being is 'this or that' means that Being *is* not. To go on holding that it may be something other than it is means stating that at the same time a datum both *is* and *is not*. Besides, if Being has 'become' this or that, then it must have come from a Being or from a non-being. If it comes from a non-being then one states an absurdity because nothing is ever created from nothing; if it comes from Being then we must agree that Being stems from

Being, which means that it remains constantly equal to itself in all its indivisibility and, in that case, one cannot speak of 'becoming', 'birth' or of finding oneself in another condition, because Being that remains identical to itself does not undergo any movement, birth or change.

One requires a certain type of understanding, not of the sensorial order, and has to consider that that which is universal, absolute and a-formal, cannot be transposed into any particular dialectical perspective, or into any kind of dogmatic rationalism. The metaphysical pathway stands upon the plane of informal intelligence, so the emotional sphere is completely excluded from it. This type of *Yoga* is the *Yoga* of the pure intuition of things and appearances, it goes beyond all phenomenology, all common reason, all kinds of religion, and changeable social morality, all sensorial experience, because all these things are the outcome of mediated knowledge. The metaphysical truth has no schemes, concepts or mental, analytical frameworks because it transcends all physical experience. On the other hand, to meditate upon what does not correspond to any sensorial datum is not easy; the sensorial mind needs to conceive all reality in relation to a form or an image, and most of the time the image itself imprisons the thinker who, on the contrary, should always be independent. The metaphysical pathway presents certain difficulties because one must abandon normal thinking processes and transfer oneself into a condition of a-dimensional, a-formal and unusual comprehension. This, obviously, requires abandoning the personal and collective unconscious.

A premature approach to this pathway might well paralyze the normal perceptive and sensorial thinking process, without leading to superior understanding. The result would be endless mental inertia and confusion, with aberrant states of consciousness giving rise to the annihilation of representative mental dynamics. This danger can be more acute here in the West because one tends to have a sensorial-formal kind of mind to which a unique and irreplaceable value is also attributed. The metaphysical way is certainly the road which *comprehends* the Infinite with its manifesting and manifest virtual possibilities; but this *comprehension* is integral Realization in that the adept has realized an effective, conscious and non-theoretical Identity (because in that case knowledge would be simply of the sensorial or rational-formal order, therefore mere erudition), which is not virtual because such a condition has always existed and has never ceased to exist. One does not arrive at *Asparśayoga* by means of self-imposed discipline, faith or devotion nor any kind of action due to individual-sensorial expression, but through a deeply inner kind of self-awareness whereby all extrovert energy tends toward its exhaustion, rendering the spirit totally *free*. Once the undivided Point has been reached, the notion of translatory movement no longer exists; the *spirit*, by eliminating the form or its own reflection being quenched, returns to its essence, devoid of cause, time and space.

Asparśayoga represents the last step and the goal of all experience and human realizative possibilities. Beyond all experience there is the 'moment' of total comprehension of our own essence; it is the maturity of perfect equilibrium and pre-existential a-condition. The ordinary individual is bound by concepts of time and space, therefore of the manifest, of evolving objects; only very few are capable of revealing that eternal present, that alpha and omega of what is commonly called change. Since the metaphysician is not satisfied with having known and transcended the limited subject-object, he dares to climb up onto the last informal step of the vibrating universal stairway to... discover himself.

Asparśayoga may be considered as the highest expression of spiritual knowledge, a kind of knowledge, or rather, of 'comprehension' by means of self-existential identification, which integrally leads from the unreal to the Real, from death to Life, from the finite to the Infinite, from the relative (human and divine) to the unqualified Absolute without a second, from illusory differentiation to supreme Identity... ».

RAPHAEL
Unity of Tradition

Having attained a synthesis of Knowledge (with which eclecticism or syncretism are not to be confused), Raphael aims at "presenting" the Universal Tradition in its many Eastern and Western expressions. He has spent a substantial number of years writing and publishing books on spiritual experience and his works include commentaries on the *Qabbālāh*, Hermeticism and Alchemy. He has also commented on and compared the Orphic Tradition with the works of Plato, Parmenides and Plotinus. Furthermore, Raphael is the author of several books on the pathway of non-duality (*Advaita*), which he has translated from the original Sanskrit, offering commentaries on a number of key Vedantic texts.

With reference to Platonism, Raphael has highlighted the fact that, if we were to draw a parallel between Śaṅkara's *Advaita Vedānta* and a Traditional Western Philosophical Vision, we could refer to the Vision presented by Plato. Drawing such a parallel does not imply a search for reciprocal influences, but rather it points to something of paramount importance: a sole Truth, inherent in the doctrines and teachings of several great thinkers, who although far apart in time and space, have reached similar and in some cases even identical conclusions.

One notices how Raphael's writes from a metaphysical perspective in order to manifest and underscore the Unity of Tradition, under the metaphysical perspective. This does not mean that he is in opposition to a dualistic perspective, or to the various religious faiths, or "points of view".

A true embodied metaphysical Vision cannot be opposed to anything. What is important for Raphael is the unveiling, through living and being, of that level of Truth which one has been able to contemplate.

Writing in the light of the Unity of Tradition Raphael's works present, calling on the reader's intuition, precise points of correspondence between Eastern and Western Teachings. These points of reference are useful for those who want to approach a comparative doctrinal study and to enter the spirit of the Unity of Teaching.

For those who follow either an Eastern or a Western traditional line these correspondences help us comprehend how the *Philosophia Perennis* (Universal Tradition), which has no history and has not been formulated by human minds as such, «comprehends universal truths that do not belong to any people or any age». It is only for lack of "comprehension" or of "synthetic vision" that one particular Branch is considered the only reliable one. Such a position can but lead to opposition and fanaticism. What can degenerate the Doctrine is either a sentimental, fanatical devotion or condescending intellectualism, which is critical and sterile, dogmatic and separative.

In Raphael's words: «For those of us who aim at Realization, our task is to get to the essence of every Doctrine, because we know that just as Truth is one, so Tradition is one even if, just like Truth, Tradition may be viewed from a plurality of apparently different points of view. We must abandon all disquisitions concerning the phenomenal process of becoming, and move onto the plane of Being. In other words: we must have a Philosophy of Being as the foundation of our search and of our realization»[1].

Raphael interprets spiritual practice as a "Path of Fire". Here is what he writes: «...The "Path of Fire" is the pathway each disciple follows in all branches of Tradition; it is the Way of Return. Therefore, it is not the particular teaching of an individual nor a path parallel to the one and only Main Road... After all, every disciple follows his own "Path of Fire", no matter which Branch of Tradition he belongs to».

---

[1] See, Raphael, *Tat tvam asi*, That thou art, Aurea Vidyā, New York.

In Raphael's view, what is important is to express through living and being the truth that one has been able to contemplate. Thus, for each being, one's expression of thought and action must be coherent and in agreement with one's own specific *dharma*.

After more than thirty-five years of teaching, both oral and written, Raphael is now dedicating himself only to those people who wish to be "doers" rather than "sayers", according to St. Paul's expression.

Raphael is connected with the *maṭha* founded by *Śrī Ādi* Śaṅkara at Śṛṅgeri and Kāñcīpuram as well as with the Rāmaṇa Āśram at Tiruvannamalai.

Founder of the Āśram Vidyā Order, he now dedicates himself entirely to spiritual practice. He lives in a hermitage connected to the *āśram* and devotes himself completely to a vow of silence.

* * *

May Raphael's Consciousness, expression of Unity of Tradition, guide and illumine along this Opus all those who donate their *mens informalis* (non-formal mind) to the attainment of the highest known Realization.

PUBLICATIONS

Books by Raphael
published in English

At the Source of Life
Aurea Vidyā, New York

Beyond the illusion of the ego
Aurea Vidyā, New York

Essence and purpose of Yoga
The Initiatory Pathways to the Transcendent
Element Books, Shaftesbury, U.K.

Initiation into the Philosophy of Plato
Aurea Vidyā, New York

Orphism and the Initiatory Tradition
Aurea Vidyā, New York

The Pathway of Fire according to the Qabbālāh
'Ehjeh 'Ašer 'Ehjeh (I am That I am)
Aurea Vidyā, New York

The Pathway of Non-duality, Advaitavāda
Motilal Banarsidass, New Delhi

The Science of Love
Aurea Vidyā, New York

Tat tvam asi, That thou art,
The Path of Fire According to the Asparśavāda
Aurea Vidyā, New York

The Threefold Pathway of Fire
Aurea Vidyā, New York

Traditional Classics
in English

Śaṅkara, *Ātmabodha*∗, Self-knowledge.
Aurea Vidyā, New York

Bhagavadgītā, The Celestial Song∗.
Aurea Vidyā, New York

Śaṅkara, *Drigdriśyaviveka*∗,
Discernment between *ātman* and non-*ātman*.
Aurea Vidyā, New York

Gauḍapāda, *Māṇḍūkyakārikā*∗,
The *Māṇḍūkya Upaniṣad* with the verses-*kārikā* of Gauḍapāda.
Aurea Vidyā, New York

Parmenides, *On the Order of Nature*, Περί φύσεως∗∗, For a Philosophical Ascesis.
Aurea Vidyā, New York

Śaṅkara, *Vivekacūḍāmaṇi*∗, The Crest-jewel of Discernment.
Aurea Vidyā, New York

Forthcoming Publications
in English

Patañjali, *The Regal Way to Realization*∗, Yogadarśana

Śaṅkara, *Aparokṣānubhūti*∗, Self-realization

Bādarāyaṇa, *Brahmasūtra*∗

Five Upaniṣads∗, Īśa, Kaivalya, Sarvasāra, Amṛtabindu, Atharvaśira

∗ Translated from the Sanskrit, and Commented, by Raphael
∗∗ Edited by Raphael

Aurea Vidyā is the Publishing House of the Parmenides Traditional Philosophy Foundation, a Not-for-Profit Organization whose purpose is to make Perennial Philosophy accessible.

The Foundation goes about its purpose in a number of ways: by publishing and distributing Traditional Philosophy texts with Aurea Vidyā, by offering individual and group encounters and by providing a Reading Room and daily Meditations at its Center.

* * *

Those readers who have an interest in Traditional Philosophy are welcome to contact the Foundation at: parmenides.foundation@earthlink.net.